Penguins

·ALL··ABOUT··ANIMALS·

Penguins

by Jane Arlington and Sharon Langdon

Reader's Digest

YOUNG FAMILIES

Published by The Reader's Digest Association Limited

London • New York • Sydney • Montreal

CONTENTS

Chapter 1

A penguin story

It's the first day of winter on the continent of Antarctica. A group of emperor penguins huddles together for warmth. The penguins chatter and whistle excitedly. Any day now, the mother penguins will be ready to lay their eggs.

After Mummy Penguin lays her egg, Daddy Penguin rolls it carefully with his beak from her webbed feet on to his own.

Then he covers the precious bundle under a special feathered flap to keep it safe and warm. He says goodbye to Mummy Penguin, who sets off on a very long walk to the sea to find food.

Daddy Penguin shuffles inside the huddle, taking great care not to let the egg roll off his feet. Two months later, it is time for Little Penguin to hatch.

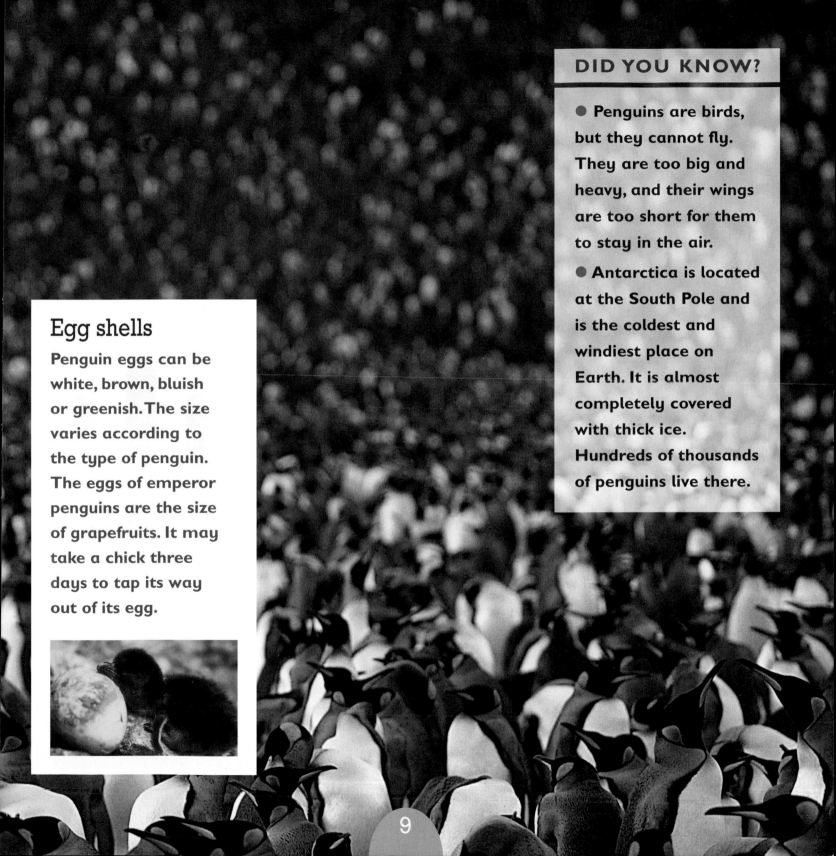

Egg shells

Penguin eggs can be white, brown, bluish or greenish. The size varies according to the type of penguin. The eggs of emperor penguins are the size of grapefruits. It may take a chick three days to tap its way out of its egg.

When Mummy Penguin comes back with food from the sea, she calls out to Daddy Penguin by singing a song. It is the song she sang to him the first time they met. When he sings back, she is able to find him and their baby in the crowded colony. Little Penguin is peeking out from his special place on his father's feet. The family is back together again.

Little Penguin grows very quickly. Soon he is too big to stay on his parents' feet. He joins a group of other penguin chicks, snuggling closely with them to stay safe and warm. Meanwhile, adult penguins keep a watchful eye on them.

Little Penguin's mother shows him how to use his beak to clean his feathers. The chicks are covered with a special layer of fine, fluffy, soft feathers called 'down'.

Feet first

After baby penguins hatch from their eggs, they stay in a special place on their father's feet called a 'brood patch', where it is cosy and warm under the feathers. It has a great view, too.

After a few months, Little Penguin and the rest of the penguin chicks have grown enough waterproof feathers to be allowed into the water.

They follow their parents on a long walk to the sea where they will learn to catch fish. It is fun to slide down the snowy hills on their stomachs.

When they reach the water, Little Penguin jumps in with his friends. The penguin chicks are not good swimmers at first. They watch how the grown-ups use their webbed feet and stiff wings like the oars of a boat to push through the water. Soon the chicks are diving and 'flying' through the water, just like their parents.

The penguins spend many weeks by the sea, eating. When the air turns colder, they know winter is coming. By now, Little Penguin is no longer a baby. He looks just like his parents but a bit shorter.

In a few years, Little Penguin will become an adult himself – and balance an egg of his own on his feet.

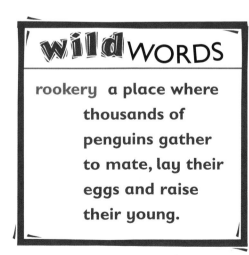

wildWORDS

rookery a place where thousands of penguins gather to mate, lay their eggs and raise their young.

Chapter 2

Comical and amazing

A penguin's webbed feet
help it to steer through the
water. Its sharp claws grip
the icy ground.

16

Penguin portrait

There are many different kinds of penguins living in different parts of the world, but they are all very much alike. They have black or dark blue backs and white undersides. Because they stand upright on their short, wide legs and webbed feet, many people think penguins look like little men wearing tailcoats.

Cooling off

Penguins are warm-blooded. Their body temperature is almost the same as yours. When they feel too hot, penguins extend their wings. This allows the extra heat to escape from both sides of their wings.

Penguins have other physical traits in common:

● The beak, or bill, is short and sharp — good for catching fish.

● The wings are short and the bones inside are flat to keep them from bending as the penguins push themselves through the water.

● The puffy chest contains strong muscles that provide power to the wings.

● The tail is used for balance on land and for steering in the water.

● A pocket inside the penguin's throat, called a crop, stores food.

● A flap of skin and feathers, called a brood patch, keeps the egg, and later the chick, warm and insulated.

Looking good

Feather fluff

Penguins moult – lose their feathers – once a year and then grow new feathers. It takes three weeks for the new feathers to grow. During this time, a penguin can't go into the water and so it doesn't eat. It uses up a lot of energy while moulting, often losing half its body weight.

Like most birds, penguins clean their feathers regularly. This activity is called 'preening'. Preening is especially important for penguins after they have been in the water. Diving pushes the air out of their feathers, flattening them.

Penguins then need to fluff their feathers up to help trap their body heat. As they preen, penguins rub oil onto their feathers with their beak to make them waterproof. The oil is made in a gland near the tail.

Preening helps penguins keep their feathers windproof and waterproof.

DID YOU KNOW?

Some penguins sleep standing up. They may tuck their head under a wing. Penguins can also go to sleep in the water.

19

Breathing underwater

Penguins cannot breathe underwater. They have to come to the surface to breathe in air. Penguins can swim for long distances and for long periods of time by leaping gracefully above the water to breathe and then diving back in; dolphins and porpoises breathe in the same way.

Most penguins have to come up for air quite often, so their dives are short and shallow. The emperor penguin is different. It has small stones in its stomach that help it to be a champion diver. With this extra weight, it can dive up to 20 metres, holding its breath for 18 minutes to catch squid and fish.

With their stiff wings and fast speed, penguins look as if they are flying through the water.

Birds that swim

DID YOU KNOW?

- **Penguins have two layers of feathers that help them to stay warm in freezing cold water. The outer layer of waterproof feathers keeps their skin dry. The inner layer traps warm air against their bodies. Beneath the feathers a layer of fat, called 'blubber', offers additional protection.**

- **The penguin's body colours help to keep it safe in the water. Its white underside is difficult for a predator to see from below. Its dark back makes the penguin difficult to see from above.**

Penguins can't fly, but they are super swimmers. They are heavier than flying birds, so they can dive below the ocean's surface. Penguins have a sleek, streamlined shape that glides easily through the water. Their tail and webbed feet help them to steer. Stiff wings act like paddles, pushing the penguins forward.

Penguins move more quickly in water than they do on land. Their average swimming speed is about 15 miles per hour – four times faster than a human swimmer.

On the move

Penguins spend most of their lives in the ocean. The rest of the time they are on land, travelling to and from or staying at their rookery – the place penguins mate and raise their young.

Since penguins don't fly, how do they get from the water onto land? Where the coastline is like a beach, penguins can simply walk onto land. But when the coast is rocky or high because of snow and ice, the penguins jump straight out of the water and land flat on their feet, like cats. Adélie penguins are only 60 centimetres tall, but they can leap three times that high to get from the water onto land.

On snowy terrain, penguins 'toboggan' – they slide on their bellies, using their wings and feet like ski poles to push themselves down hills and across the snow, often for miles and miles. During long journeys, penguins take turns being first. The leader flops onto its stomach and makes a track in the snow, which the others follow. This saves energy, because the other penguins don't need to create tracks for themselves.

DID YOU KNOW?

Penguins can stand upright because their legs are set so far back on their bodies, unlike the legs of other birds.

Penguins frequently march in long, regular lines like soldiers. They walk with their webbed feet flat on the icy ground, swaying slightly from side to side. This waddling effect can look very comical.

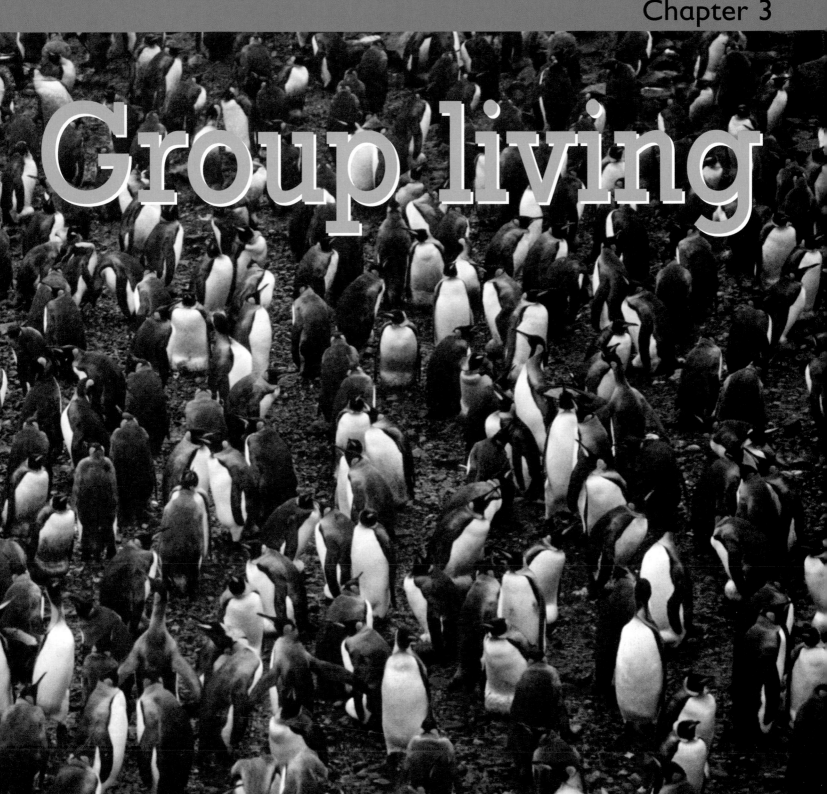

Group living

DID YOU KNOW?

Different species of penguins use different sorts of sounds, such as trumpeting, cooing, singing and croaking. Parents and chicks also recognise each other by sight.

26

Huddling for warmth

In the southern half of the world where penguins live, the seasons are the opposite of what they are here in the Northern Hemisphere. For the thousands of penguins living in Antarctica, the harsh and terrible winter begins in May and ends around September. Summer begins in October or November and ends in February or March.

Living in large groups helps penguins to stay warm. Emperor penguins form huddles during the fierce and freezing winter weather. They take turns standing in the middle, where it is warmest, and on the outside, where it is coldest. The temperature inside a huddle can be more than 20°C – like a mild summer's day. When it is really cold, penguins huddle very close together, reducing the amount of heat they lose by as much as 50 per cent.

The crowded huddle also makes it possible for penguins to survive on the limited amount of land suitable for them. Penguin colonies are like cities where humans live, with hundreds of thousands of birds sharing the space. And, because penguins communicate with their voices, imagine how noisy penguin colonies can be.

Safety in numbers

Being in a huge group greatly increases an individual penguin's chances of survival against predators. While one penguin on its own wouldn't seem very frightening to an attacker, thousands of penguins together are quite an army.

Seals, sea lions, sharks and killer whales all hunt penguins in the water. On land, penguins are hunted by foxes and snakes. One of the main threats to penguins is water pollution by humans.

Penguin eggs and babies are sometimes attacked by birds that swoop down from the air. These birds usually choose chicks that have strayed from the group or that are weak or sickly.

Thousands of pairs of eyes are better than one pair when it comes to spotting attackers.

Beak defence

When penguins see a bird flying in to attack, they raise an alarm call to the colony. At once, thousands of beaks turn upward to the sky. Faced with such a pointed defence, the attackers usually fly away.

Sea food

Penguins eat only when they are at sea and not when on land. Penguins in zoos have to be specially trained to eat when out of water.

They eat krill – tiny, shrimplike creatures – crabs, squid, fish and whatever else they can find in the ocean.

Their appetites are huge as swimming uses up a lot of energy. Adélie penguins, for instance, eat an average of one shrimp every 6 seconds.

Penguins don't have teeth. They swallow their food whole. Their tongues are spiny and their jaws are strong, allowing them to hang onto slippery fish.

Unlike humans, penguins can drink salty seawater without becoming ill. Special glands at the tips of their beaks remove the salt, which then flows down grooves to the end of their beaks and drips off.

Jumping in

When a group of penguins reaches the the edge of the ice they don't always rush straight into the water, even if they are very hungry. Often, one brave bird goes first to make sure the water is safe and no predator is nearby to attack them. Then the rest jump in, sometimes all at once.

Chapter 4

Parents and chicks

Egg sitter

Penguin dads, like this rockhopper father, keep their eggs safe and warm until the baby penguin is hatched.

Mother and father penguins share the responsibility of raising their little ones.

One in a million

How does a penguin find its mate among the thousands of identical-looking penguins in the rookery? By listening for its mate's song. Every penguin has its own song, which its mate can recognise.

When the pair meet, they stand facing each other, raise their beaks in the air and weave their heads back and forth together.

Going home

Every year, penguins return to the place where they were born – to moult and change their feathers, mate, lay their eggs and raise their young. Some penguins must travel great distances to their home. Adélie penguins have walked more than 200 miles to reach their breeding ground. Scientists believe that penguins use the position of the sun, stars and familiar places along the way to find their home.

Usually, the males arrive first to stake out their nesting site, which is sometimes a patch of ground only the size of a bath mat. Most penguins build nests on the ground, using pebbles, sticks, grass and seaweed. Others build nests underground. Emperor penguins do not make nests at all. The father penguin puts the egg on his feet and keeps it safe and warm in a special place under his feathers called a 'brood patch'.

Penguin chicks

After hatching from the eggs, penguin chicks stay on their parents' feet for warmth and protection. By the time they are about seven weeks old, most chicks have grown too big to remain with their parents. They join a nursery group of 20 or more other young penguins, called a 'crèche', where they huddle together for warmth. In some species, the crèche is guarded by several adult penguins on the lookout for predators.

Young penguins are completely dependent on their parents for food – even after they have grown too big to stand on their parents' feet. They cannot enter the water until their fluffy down feathers are replaced by grown-up ones. This can be as short as seven weeks or as long as 13 months. Once the chick has fledged, or grown its adult feathers, it can go into the water to feed for itself.

Feed me

A penguin chick's parents take turns going to the sea and bringing back food for their baby. The parent stores the food in its crop, a pocket inside the penguin's throat specially for this purpose. The parent brings the food back up from its crop directly into the chick's mouth.

When young penguins are too big to stay on their parents' feet, they huddle together in a small group.

Chapter 5

Penguins in the world

Adélie penguins are named after Adélie Dumont d'Urville, the wife of the Frenchman who explored Antarctica. They are the smallest penguins living in the Antarctic – 45 to 60 centimetres high – and weigh about 5 kilograms.

Crazy feathers

Rockhopper penguins are named for the way they move around – hopping from rock to rock. They have a crest of feathers on the top of their heads with a plume of yellow ones. Rockhoppers live on the rocky islands of the sub-Antarctic and on warmer islands in the Indian and south Atlantic oceans.

All kinds of penguins

There are 17 different kinds of penguins.

Emperor penguins are the largest. They are 90 to 100 centimetres high and weigh 30 to 40 kilograms. They live only in Antarctica where temperatures can be -60°C and the winds more than 100 miles per hour.

King penguins are the second largest and look a lot like emperor penguins. Kings have bright yellow feathers on their chest. They are about 95 centimetres high and weigh about 15 kilograms. King penguins live on the sub-Antarctic and Antarctic islands.

Little Blues are the smallest of all the penguins. They are only about 30 centimetres high and weigh just 1 kilogram. Little Blues can be found only in Australia and New Zealand. Of all the penguins, they sing the most.

Galápagos penguins live on the hot, tropical island of Galápagos, off the coast of Ecuador in South America, where the temperature can be more than 38°C. These penguins are about 55 centimetres high and weigh 3 kilograms.

Chinstrap penguins are named after the black line that runs under their chin. They also have pink feet. Chinstraps stand about 75 centimetres high and weigh about 5 kilograms. These penguins live only in the Antarctic.

Where penguins live

All penguins live in the Southern Hemisphere, below the Earth's equator. Many live where it is icy and freezing cold. But others live where the temperature is mild or even tropical.

Penguins are sea birds. They spend most of their life in the water, which is where they eat. Once a year, they return to the place where they were born to moult their feathers and raise their baby chicks.

Emperor penguins, the largest penguin species, live all their lives in the icy Antarctic in colonies varying in size from several hundred to tens of thousands of birds.

FAST FACTS ABOUT EMPEROR PENGUINS

SCIENTIFIC NAME	*Aptenodytes forsteri*
CLASS	Aves
ORDER	Sphenisciformes
WEIGHT	27kg to 40kg
HEIGHT	Just under or just over 1 metre
EGGS	1 each year
SWIMMING SPEED	15 miles per hour
LIFE SPAN	Up to 20 years
HABITAT	Ocean, coastline of ice-covered Antarctica

GLOSSARY OF Wild WORDS

blubber	a layer of fat under the skin of sea animals that keeps them warm
breeding ground	a place where animals go to mate, give birth and raise their young
chick	a young penguin
crèche	a group of young penguins huddling together for protection and warmth
crop	a pocket inside a penguin's throat to store food
down	soft and fluffy feathers
equator	an imaginary line around the Earth that is halfway between the North Pole and the South Pole

flipper	a wide flat limb used for swimming
gland	a part of the body that makes chemicals an animal needs to live
hatch	to be born by breaking out of an egg
huddle	a very big group of penguins
incubation	the time spent warming an egg until it hatches
krill	a tiny shrimplike creature living in the sea that penguins eat
migrate	to go from one place to another at certain times of the year to find food or to mate and give birth

moult	to shed old feathers and grow new ones	regurgitate	to bring swallowed food back into the mouth
pollution	something harmful or poisonous that makes water or air less pure	rookery	a place where thousands of penguins gather to mate, lay their eggs and raise their young
predator	an animal that hunts and eats other animals	skua	an arctic bird that eats penguin eggs and chicks
preen	to groom feathers or fur with a beak or tongue	terrain	ground or land
prey	an animal that is hunted by another for food	warm-blooded	having a body temperature that stays the same even when the outside temperature changes

45

INDEX

CREDITS

Penguins is an *All About Animals* fact book
published by Reader's Digest Young Families, Inc.

Written by Jane Arlington and Sharon Langdon

Copyright © 2005 Reader's Digest Young Families, Inc.
This edition was adapted and published in 2008 by
The Reader's Digest Association Limited
11 Westferry Circus, Canary Wharf, London E14 4HE
® Reader's Digest, the Pegasus logo and Reader's Digest Young Families
are registered trademarks of
The Reader's Digest Association, Inc.

We are committed to both the quality of our products and the service we provide to our customers.
We value your comments, so please feel free to contact us on
08705 113366 or via our website at: www.readersdigest.co.uk
If you have any comments or suggestions about the content of our books,
you can contact us at: gbeditorial@readersdigest.co.uk

Printed in China

Book code: 640-003 UP0000-1
ISBN: 978 0 276 44320 6

For Ameli
x x X

First published 2007 by Macmillan Children's Books
a division of Macmillan Publishers Limited
20 New Wharf Road, London N1 9RR
Basingstoke and Oxford
Associated companies throughout the world
www.panmacmillan.com

ISBN: 978-1-4050-8949-4

Text and illustrations copyright © Emily Gravett 2007

The right of Emily Gravett to be identified as the author and
illustrator of this work has been asserted by her in accordance
with the Copyright, Designs and Patents Act 1988.

3 5 7 9 8 6 4 2

A CIP catalogue record for this book is available from the British Library.

Printed in China

Emily Gravett

Macmillan Children's Books

Monkey and me,
Monkey and me,
Monkey and me,
We went to see,

We went to see some . . .

PENGUINS!

Monkey and me,

Monkey and me,

Monkey and me,

We went to see,

We went to see some . . .

KANGA

ROOS!

Monkey and me,
Monkey and me,
Monkey and me,
We went to see,

We went to see some . . .

BATS!

Monkey and me,
Monkey and me,
Monkey and me,
We went to see,

We went to see some . . .

ELEPHANTS!

Monkey and me,

Monkey and me,

Monkey and me,

We went to see,

We went to see some . . .

KEYS!

Monkey . . . and . . . me,

Monkey . . . and . . . me,

Monkey . . . and . . . me,

We went . . .

. . . home for tea.